An Animal Shelter's Guide to

FUNDRAISING

A How-To Guide for Creating a Strategic Fundraising Plan

Tim Crum

Foreword by Merritt Clifton

PRAISE FOR
Tim Crum and *An Animal Shelter's Guide to Fundraising*

"Tim is one of the few top professionals who can "do" and "teach".   This book is for anyone who does or plans on doing any fundraising. Whether you are just beginning or you have been doing it for a while, there is something to learn for everyone. This is the best and most complete book I have read on fundraising as it walks you through from start to finish. I especially love the "activity stars", if you stop and do each activity not only will you have a fundraising plan at the end but equally important is that you will know more about your organization and your donors.   Opening a nonprofit where you exist on donations and grants 100% is quite a leap - since reading this book our organization has begun to implement its lessons and we are more confident than ever that we will reach our goals."

> - Katherine Johnson, President & Founder
>   Friends for Animals Sanctuary, Inc., Melbourne, FL

"Finally! We know we have to do it, but how to do it has always been the hard part *until now*. *An Animals Shelter's Guide to Fundraising* provides the what, where, when, who and how to fundraising. As you read, Tim carefully guides you through the preparation of several important exercises. If you complete the exercises as you read, when you are finished you have a workable plan, designed for your organization, and can immediately put what you learned to work. It's the perfect guidebook for the busy board member, volunteer or anyone looking to raise more funds for an animal shelter."

> - Kathleen Toth, Esq., Board Member
>   Friends of Animals Utah,   Park City, UT

"To think of all the time and effort I could have saved if I'd had this book years ago! Tim Crum has successfully compiled years of experience and know-how into an easy-to-understand guide on one of the most daunting tasks of running a nonprofit organization to help the animals. Creating a well-organized plan to raise funds is critical to ensuring you can serve the animals in your community for now and years to come. This book is a "must read" for any animal welfare professional or volunteer tasked with raising dollars."

> - Jill Tucker, Executive Director
>   Santa Maria Valley Humane Society, Santa Maria, CA

"This is truly a great book for people who want to "get there from here."

> - Ruth Steinberger, Director
>   Spay First, Oklahoma City, OK

"Tim has created an easy to understand, how-to guide to help fundraisers at any level, raise funds for animals in need. This is a must-have guide for animal welfare organizations, large or small."

- Nadine Walmsley, Nonprofit Fundraising Professional
Chicago, IL

"Tim's book does a great job of guiding the reader through the thought process involved in planning for a successful fundraising campaign."

- Jaydeen Vincente, Founder and Board Member
Animal Shelter to Riverbank & Oakdale, Oakdale, CA

"Running an animal shelter can be overwhelming. A 'typical' day may include backed up drains in the kennels, staffing issues, meetings with community members, paying bills, writing thank you letters and more. On top of the day-to-day activities, there is always the feeling that you're not doing enough to raise funds to support your mission. *An Animal Shelter's Guide to Fundraising* is an excellent tool to evaluate your fundraising efforts and plan for the future. I encourage anyone in animal welfare to invest the time necessary to read this book, complete the workbook and produce an actionable plan."

- Mary Beth Wegener, Executive Director
Olympic Peninsula Humane Society, Port Angeles, WA

"*An Animal Shelter's Guide to Fundraising* gets to the point. Tim Crum's book takes the reader through steps in the fundraising process for successful financial outcomes. With years of experience in the field, Crum offers valuable tools for both shelters and rescues that do not have access to professional fundraisers."

- Debra J. White, Animal Advocate
Phoenix, AZ

"Any shelter or rescue organization looking for expert guidance on setting up a successful fund raising program need look no further. Tim Crum's passion for animal welfare and his experience as a successful fund raiser in the shelter world makes him the perfect guide. Having a well-organized plan is half the battle to raising all the money your organization needs, and Tim helps you develop the plan that is right for you. He leads you through all the required steps and helps you understand the importance of each exercise you complete. Along the way, you're building your campaign. Get started! There's money to be raised!"

- Julie Duke, Executive Director
PEDIGREE Foundation, Nashville, TN

Copies of this book are available from the author at discount when purchased in quantity for conferences, workshops or for an entire organization.

Published by
Shark Press Publishing
12425 West Bell Road
Suite 117
Surprise AZ 85378
Tel: 623.975.1234

Disclaimer
The information contained within this book is for informational purposes. The intent and purpose of this information is to prepare you for the development of a strategic fundraising plan. We make no guarantees or warranties regarding the results of your fundraising activity. Fundraising results may vary from person to person dependent upon the individual's skill, experience, effort, resources, donors, strategy, tactics and activity. Neither the publisher nor author shall be liable for any loss of profit or any other damages.

Dedication

An Animal Shelter's Guide to Fundraising is dedicated to the life and memory of Paul Jolly, a friend and mentor.

Acknowledgement

I would like to thank my first (and best) boss in fundraising, Lisa C. Young, CFRE, for being the epitome of a dedicated fundraising professional. I have always admired Lisa's fundraising knowledge, experience, enthusiasm and ethics. She set the first and highest standard for me as a fundraising professional. Her influence is a standard that I constantly strive to meet in my career.

Thanks also to Peter Casella for hiring me as the director of development and public relations at the Animal Rescue League in Pittsburgh, PA. After ten years as a fundraiser in higher education and healthcare, Peter recognized the combination of my fundraising skills and passion for animals was a unique mixture that could help advance the mission of the organization. He was a wonderful mentor and boss. He knew precisely when to let my skills shine and when to guide my raw talent. Under his leadership, I grew and developed both as a professional and as an individual. I am forever grateful that he hired me. It started my career in a field I am very passionate about.

The author thanks Kim Venturo for editing this book. Acknowledgement to Lena Flores and the team at Graphic Ideals for taking my book cover ideas and making them beautiful front and back cover designs.

To all the co-workers, fundraising professionals, and client-partners who have been a part of my journey – far too many to name individually – thank you for helping me in some way, small or big, as it helped shape my career and ultimately this book.

To my parents who always filled our household with dogs. My love and connection to pets was instilled at the earliest age and provided for many wonderful childhood memories.

To all the pets who have been part of my life and have loved me unconditionally. Zelda, Nugget, Jordan, Buddy, Two Socks, Bocelli, Daisy, Pebbles and Kibbles. They have enriched my life and continue to inspire me to help homeless pets.

And especially to my wife, Kristen, and my children, Olivia and Jack without whose love, smiles, patience and encouragement, this book would not exist.

Table of Contents

Table of Contents

Foreword

Close to 20 years have elapsed since the debut of the original No Kill Conference series, held annual from 1995 through 2005 by the long defunct organization Doing Things for Animals, sponsored primarily by the North Shore Animal League America.

There were at that time a few large well-funded no-kill shelters, most notably North Shore, but even the Best Friends Animal Society, now the third most affluent sheltering charity in the world, was then still relatively small and struggling. The high-volume direct mail fundraising and public relations strategies that worked for North Shore required up-front input that was beyond the means of most of the participants in the first No Kill Conferences.

Looking around for people who could teach fundraising and public relations for shelter directors operating on budgets of nothing, the No Kill Conference organizers drafted me, Tim Crum, and Bonney Brown.

Bonney had demonstrated that different fundraising approaches could succeed anywhere. Since the MSPCA and Animal Rescue League had never held fundraising dog walks, Bonney organized the biggest fundraising dog walks ever held anywhere, to that time, and taught hundreds of other humane society fundraisers how to make dog walks a productive activity.

My contribution came from the experience of having worked in news media since my mid-teens, often reporting about nonprofit accountability. I had a reasonable idea what colleagues in the news racket would read and amplify, and of what donors would expect to see by way of progress reports and statistics.

That left everything else having to do with bringing in money up to Tim.

Tim, then as now, emphasized planning. *An Animal Shelter's Guide to Fundraising* offers relatively little of the technical details of producing direct mail campaigns, organizing special events such as dog walks, and raising funds online. These, after all, involve skills that can be learned almost anywhere in the nonprofit sector. Instead, Tim explains specifically for animal shelter directors how to identify potential donors, how to hone a fundraising message that will appeal specifically to potential donors to an animal charity, and how to set up a fundraising cycle, that will keep the money coming in year-round, whereas far too many shelters (and shelterless rescues) tend to lurch perpetually from feast to famine and back again, until they and their leadership collapse under the stress of continually coping with crisis.

The extent to which successful fundraising depends on planning tends to elude most people who have not done much fundraising. Yet planning is the first aspect of fundraising that professional fundraisers talk about. Direct mail appeals, both passive and active electronic fundraising campaigns, and the success of special events all depend upon timing almost as much as upon what is actually said. Well-timed campaigns, using multiple methods and media, tend to reinforce each other. An effective donor acquisition strategy rolls over into effective donor retention, and eventually into effectively soliciting bequests.

Tim also emphasizes the importance of enabling caring people to help. As much as Tim says about this, more needs to be said.

Many effective but impoverished animal charities do not get the support they need simply because they do not ask enough people for help, or ask often enough--or they spend their fundraising time chasing elusive foundation grants, instead of developing their own donor base.

Many of the hardest-working, most honest, and most devotedly compassionate people who are doing humane work are inhibited about making their needs known--especially locally, where others are most able to help, as volunteers and as donors of goods and services, even if they have no money to give.

Animal charity directors often behave as if they themselves are feral cats and street dogs, doomed to scavenge, in constant danger from a kick, stoning, or impoundment if they approach anyone who might say "No."

Many others ask for help under the illusion that fundraising is begging, that only the affluent should be asked to donate, and that aid will only be given if the beggar seems poorer and more miserable than everyone else on the street.

These animal charity directors are embarrassed to present a professional image while soliciting help, and to be seen giving their animals the best of care, because they fear others will misinterpret this as meaning that they are rich, and do not really need or deserve aid.

Such attitudes are not only self-defeating but dead wrong, as shown by the ongoing success of the richest organizations. The most successful fundraisers not only attract more aid from the wealthy but also get generous help from some of the people with the least to give.

Successful fundraising, especially in poor communities, requires the charity to project itself as a center of community pride, to which everyone contributes and from which everyone derives benefit.

The most important benefit that successful charities confer is the feeling of hope that adverse conditions can be changed.

Fundraising is not begging. It is inviting fellow citizens to join in providing an essential community service. The animal charity director who asks for help should seek money, volunteers, supplies, and services with the same pride of purpose that built the world's great temple cities.

Any community that supports a church, a school, a hospital, or athletics has the means and public spirit to support a good animal shelter. What is required is selling the idea, which requires working in a manner that visibly invites participation.

The animal charity that does not ask for help, and does not enable others to assist in any way they can, is failing itself and failing the animals it seeks to aid, because it is not empowering fellow citizens and animal lovers to respond to cruelty and misery that is often breaking their hearts, because they feel that no one else cares.

Thousands of people who feel just as badly on behalf of suffering animals as the people who run animal charities are miserable every time they see a street dog or feral cat or hear about cruelty, not only because the animals are suffering, but also because they feel utterly helpless and frustrated about it.

These kind people want to do something, but will never know what to do, or how to do it, or whom to trust, until they are shown an example of someone else helping and are asked to participate, by giving money, food, transportation, volunteer time, or whatever else they have to spare that can be of use.

If all a person can do is help to socialize puppies and kittens by cuddling them for an hour that is a positive contribution, and needs to be invited, accepted, and welcomed.

Often this will lead to larger contributions later, sometimes in the form of a substantial bequest.

Most people wish they could do something to combat suffering, illness, trauma, and despair on a wider scope than just fighting the portion that comes into their own lives, but they do not feel strong enough. They do not feel they have the courage or resilience that charitable work takes. Animal rescuers and defenders are often among their secret heroes. Animal charities are doing what they would do, if they could, and they will be very glad to help in whatever way they can, if they are asked, invited to participate, and thanked.

These are timeless lessons. Most of *An Animal Shelter's Guide to Fundraising* was central to Tim's message when we first shared the No Kill Conference lectern. E-mail was then still new, the World Wide Web had just debuted, and Facebook and Twitter were a decade from invention. The costs of printing and postage were significantly different relative to each other. Any specific how-to instructions from that era would long since have become obsolete and useless.

Recognizing the importance of enabling caring people to help, however, has been central to successful humane work since the dawn of animal rescue. Absorb that lesson, and most of the rest is planning.

Merritt Clifton

Committing journalism since 1968, mostly on animal-related news beats, ANIMALS 24-7 editor Merritt Clifton in 2010 received the 15th annual ProMED-mail Award for Excellence in Outbreak Reporting on the Internet for contributions to understanding the animal behavioral and cultural aspects of emerging zoonotic disease. News editor for the Animals' Agenda magazine, 1988-1992, editor of the ANIMAL PEOPLE newspaper, 1992-2013, and editor of the ANIMAL PEOPLE Watchdog Report on Animal Charities, 1999-2013, Clifton was keynote speaker at the first No Kill Conference in 1995.

Preface

I wrote this book to provide everyday people working in animal welfare with a practical and easy-to-use guide that is based on actual fundraising techniques and practices. This guide book will help them do something many either fear and/or don't know how to do - fundraising.

In my career as a professional fundraiser in the animal welfare industry, I have been fortunate to travel the country and visit with many professionals in animal sheltering organizations from rural to urban, large to small, open admission to limited admission to no kill, North to South and East to West. Through all the years, there has been one constant. A large majority of animal shelters and rescue groups operate without any type of fundraising plan. Having been a fundraiser for my entire professional career, I can tell you that fundraising without a plan is definitely not the best way to run your organization, or your fundraising program. Quite frankly, it's a formula for failure that will place an awful lot of stress on those who do the fundraising.

In fact, not only are many organizations operating without a fundraising plan, but fundraising is usually a lower priority for them. This typically results in fundraising that is reactive and emergency-based. The consequence is an organization struggling with day-to-day finances.

Having walked a mile in your shoes, so to speak, I decided to put onto paper the systematic approach to fundraising I've used my entire professional fundraising career. This system has **guided me to achieve success in every animal welfare organization** I've worked whether it was a small, rural humane society to a large, inner city shelter, or even for one of the nation's largest national animal charity. It's the very system I use with clients and the same one I have taught hundreds of times in various cities across the country. Plain and simple – the system works and people like it.

This book's progressive approach makes it particularly easy for someone without any fundraising knowledge or background to gradually develop all of the pieces needed for a functional and effective fundraising plan. As you are guided through the book, you will notice a star at the top of those pages in which you will be asked to complete an exercise. Take the time necessary to complete these exercises. They are designed to help you every step of the way. Every exercise builds on the previous one. If you take the time to complete all the exercises, you will finish this book having drafted a functional and effective fundraising plan that will help you grow a stable and robust fundraising program.

Best wishes for much success in your journey. It's going to take some work on your part, but I know you can do it!

Tim

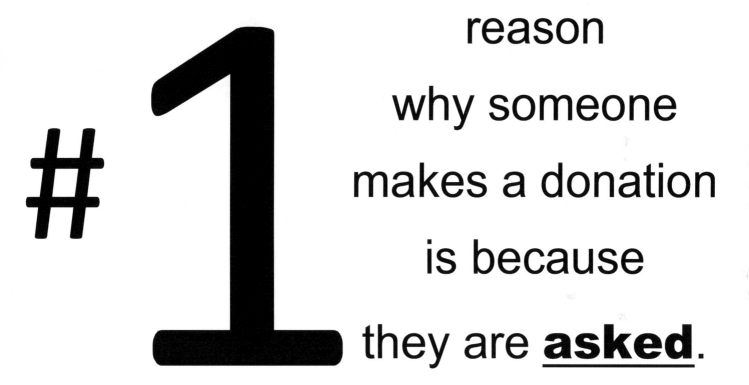

\# 1 reason why someone makes a donation is because they are **asked**.

Why You Need a Fundraising Plan (or Why We Use Road Maps)

Chances are that you got into animal welfare because you love animals so much that you wanted to take action to do something to help them. What better place to invest your time, energy and skills than by working for an animal shelter?

Yet, there are so many animal-related tasks to handle on any given day that it may be difficult, even overwhelming, to think of anything but animal care. From cleaning and disinfecting animal kennels and cages to the feeding and exercise of animals in your facility to their medical care - the animals require a lot of your time and attention. On top of all of these tasks you still have to handle a myriad of other tasks such as lost and found pets, animal adoptions, animal intake, counseling, phone calls, volunteers, posting photos of adoptable pets on social media sites, the list goes on. It's no wonder that for many small to medium sized animal sheltering organizations fundraising is usually reactive or emergency-based. The typical result is an organization never able to dig itself out of the hole and struggling to be financially sustainable.

But it doesn't have to be this way.

I know it can be different because I have operated by the very principles I am sharing in this book. It's been the secret to my professional success.

Throughout my career as a fundraising professional for nonprofit animal welfare organizations and in my work as a consultant, I have had the privilege of travelling extensively throughout the country to visit hundreds of animal shelters from small to large, rural to urban, and from limited admission to open admission. The one constant that I have found is that those groups that have taken the time to develop and follow a fundraising plan raise far more money than those without a plan. In fact, groups following a fundraising plan, in general, accomplish more for their mission (because they are focused on specific tasks), demonstrate greater efficiency with their finances and have more donors.

Now, doesn't that sound appealing?

The truth is that creating a fundraising plan can be a time consuming process requiring participation and contributions from the board, staff and sometimes even volunteers. You can either use that as an excuse and stop reading here, or use it as motivation to do what it takes to make your organization financially successful – thereby helping more pets in the process.

Because you purchased this book, that tells me, you are a "doer" – someone who makes things happen. And with this book to guide you, you are going to make a fundraising plan and make things happen!

Your fundraising plan is your road map. It shows where you are, where you are going, and with that information you can determine what roads to take and how long it will take you to get to your destination.

Just think, the next time you need to drive to an unfamiliar place, you probably use a GPS-enabled device that provides point by point driving directions. You will be provided with information such as your estimated time of arrival, average speed, specific roads to take (often having an option of different routes), along with specific turns and exit numbers. If you follow the route (presuming your GPS is updated) you'll get to your destination. This is exactly how you should come to view your fundraising.

The sad reality is that many people in animal welfare will spend more time planning how they will get somewhere than how they will raise funds for their organization. But it's time to change our industry and help you make a plan.

So, let's start mapping out your organization's fundraising by planning where you want to go and how you will get there! We'll start with an overview of the fundraising plan you are about to create on the next page…

Structure of a Fundraising Plan

In order to map out where your organization is going with its fundraising, you will be guided in the creation of a fundraising plan. A fundraising plan is made up of three parts:

PART ONE. Message   **Pages 29-60**

The first part of your fundraising plan is built around answering one basic question,
"Why do you need money?"
This is critically important to develop because every fundraising activity you will perform for your organization is based on this answer. Having agreed upon key messages will keep the entire organization in sync not just for your fundraising activity, but also for all of your organization's outgoing communication pieces like newsletters and news releases. A simple answer will not suffice for the question above. It will require consideration of many pieces of information and we are going to guide you there in the following pages.

PART TWO. Activity   **Pages 61-70**

Now that you have articulated why your organization needs money, the second part of your plan is built around answering this question,
"How are you going to raise the money?"
This part of your fundraising plan is like using a GPS device that provides point by point driving directions including everything from estimated time of arrival to route options to exit numbers. This is a comprehensive outline of all the very specific things you will do to carry out each fundraising activity you want to do. It's your road map.

PART THREE. Goals   **Pages 71-77**

The third part of your fundraising plan concludes by answering this question,
"What is your fundraising goal?"
This is essentially the destination point of your travels. If you were using a GPS device, the destination (i.e. goal) is what you would enter into the device that provides all of the information to get you to where you want to go. The destination, or goal, is how you measure your success. If you reached your destination (goal), then you are successful.

But first, there's a detour….

Why Fundraising is so Important for Animal Shelters and Rescue Groups

The sad reality is that animal sheltering is a bad business model. You see, if most animal shelters and rescue groups in our country relied upon adoptions fees to sustain their organization, they would be bankrupt. This is because most animal sheltering organizations charge less to adopt a pet than what they invest into getting the pet ready for adoption. If your organization charges $50 for a cat adoption, but invests, on average, $55 into that cat, the organization has a $5 deficit for that pet. Do this hundreds of times in a given year and your organization is operating at a deficit just to adopt pets. Unfortunate as it is, many animal sheltering groups across the United States operate using this very paradigm.

Animal sheltering organizations rely upon this model in large part because of the mass availability of pets. According to several national sources such as the ASPCA, the National Council on Pet Population Study and Policy, and Ralston Purina, the majority of household pets are obtained from acquaintances and family members. (And most of the time those pets are free). The number of pets purchased from breeders is almost equal to the number of pets adopted from an animal shelter or rescue group. If you were to also factor in the perception of animal shelters held by many people (i.e. animal shelters are loud, smelly and dimly lit places), you begin to understand the challenges facing animal shelters.

If animal shelters and rescue groups were to begin charging fees so they could cover their costs (maybe even make a profit), most would be pricing themselves out of the market and pet adoptions would suffer. And that's one of the contributing factors why animal shelters are a poor business model.

Let's use selling widgets to illustrate this model. For our example, let's imagine we are a retail store that sells widgets. Each widget costs us $.50 to acquire with a retail price of $1.00 per widget giving us a $.50 per widget profit. If we average selling 500 widgets per day, we would have a simple profit of $250 per day. However, we also need to calculate the indirect costs (i.e. overhead) of selling these widgets to understand our true profit. Overhead costs could be everything from salaries of your widget store employees to cost of the retail space for your widget store to marketing and even utilities.

Let's assume these overhead costs:

Widget Retail Store Cost per Day

Employees' salaries per day	2@$80/day	$160.00
Lease cost per day	Avg $16.43/day *$500 per month / 30.42 days per month**	$16.44
Marketing	$5.47/day *$2,000 annual cost / 365 days)*	$5.47
Utilities	$6.57 *$200/month / 30.42 days per month**	$6.57
Widget Cost	500 widgets@ $.50/widget	$250.00
Total Cost		**$438.48**

* *(avg # of days per month)*

Therefore, our true profit per day is $61.52 ($500.00 [total sales] - $438.48 [overhead costs] or just over $.12/widget profit. Assuming the retail store is open 365 days a year, our annual profit is $22,454.80 (365 days x $61.52/profit per day). In this example, the widget retail store is a profitable business.

But what if our retail widget store only sold 400 widgets per day (assuming the overhead costs were the same)? Would your widget retail store be profitable?

The answer is NO because your total cost per day remains at $438.48 while your sales would only net $400 (800 widgets @ $1 per widget). This results in a loss of $38.48 per day. It won't be long before your business is filing bankruptcy.

The animal sheltering model is akin to the latter example of widget sales (loss of $38.48 per day). Like that example, the majority of animal sheltering organizations lose money on adoptions every day. The fees they charge for adoption is less than the cost of getting that animal adopted. A poor business model, indeed.

Calculating Your Organization's Average Cost to Adopt a Pet

Use the two charts below to help you calculate the **average** cost to prepare a dog and a cat (or other animal) for adoption. (We write average because there may be an occasion when an animal requires some extra care that falls outside what your organization typically would invest in financially). This exercise may require you to get information from others such as the executive director, an accountant and/or veterinary department.

Average Cost to Prepare a Cat for Adoption

Service / Item	Cost
Veterinary Exam	
Spay / Neuter	
Vaccination(s)	
Feline Leukemia/FIV Test	
Flea/Tick Treatment	
Deworming	
Microchip	
Collar and identification tags	
Food	
Medical Treatment	
Other	
TOTAL	$

Average Cost to Prepare a Dog for Adoption

Service / Item	Cost
Veterinary Exam	
Spay / Neuter	
Vaccination(s)	
Heartworm Test	
Flea/Tick Treatment	
Deworming	
Microchip	
Collar and identification tags	
Food	
Medical Treatment	
Other	
TOTAL	$

You may find that the average cost between female and male dogs and cats is significantly different since many places have a considerable difference between the costs of spay and neuter surgery.

Adoption Fees
Complete the charts below by inserting your organization's adoption fees.

Species	Fees (Range)
Cat	
Dog	
Other	

Adoption Fees: Profit or Loss Chart
Use the charts below to determine if your organization is profiting on pet adoptions.

Cats

Cat Adoption Fee	Avg Cost to Prepare a Cat for Adoption
$	$

Difference	$
	☐ Profit ☐ Loss

Dog

Dog Adoption Fee	Avg Cost to Prepare a Dog for Adoption
$	$

Difference	$
	☐ Profit ☐ Loss

If your organization shows a loss on both dog and cat adoptions, don't worry. This is common in animal sheltering and the very reason why I wrote that animal sheltering is a poor business model.

Earned Income vs Contributed Income

This leads us to a discussion about the two types of income available to nonprofit organizations – earned income and contributed income.

Earned income

Earned Income is comprised of any revenue generated in exchange for a service. Nonprofit animal sheltering organizations generate earned income through things such as adoptions, veterinary or spay/neuter clinics, and through thrift stores. Grants that stipulate a return service for grant funding awarded also technically qualify as a form of earned income.

Contributed Income

Contributed income is anything given without condition, i.e. donation. This includes everything from contributions to donated pet food, even items donated for your thrift store (if you operate one). Contributions to nonprofit organizations, for the most part*, are tax deductible since donors can deduct the value of any contribution they give to nonprofits from their annual income for tax purposes.

*The IRS has rules pertaining to nonprofit organizations that provide something in return for a donor's contribution (i.e. quid pro quo contribution).   A nonprofit organization is required to provide written disclosure to any donor who receives goods or services in exchange for a single payment in excess of $75. Please see *IRS Publication 1771, Charitable Contributions – Substantiation and Disclosure Requirements* and *IRS Publication 526, Charitable Contributions* for more information.

As most likely demonstrated with the exercises you completed on the preceding pages, the cost to prepare a pet for adoption exceeds the cost your organization charges for a pet adoption. **Adoption fees fall under the category of earned income**.

This is the very reason why animal sheltering organizations need to focus on fundraising (Contributed Income). Contributed income allows the majority of animal sheltering organizations in our country to remain viable by off-setting losses incurred from earned income (i.e. adoptions).

Understanding Where the Money Comes From

In order to maximize your fundraising efforts, it is important to understand who (what source) is providing funds to nonprofit organizations. According to *Giving USA 2014: The Annual Report on Philanthropy for the Year 2013*, charitable contributions in 2013 by category:

Category	Percent
Individuals	72 %
Foundations	15 %
Bequests	8 %
Corporations	5 %

This data clearly demonstrates that individuals make up the majority of donor dollars. Factoring in the additional 8% in funding from bequests, you can see that 80% of all funding is coming from individuals. This tells us that the "individuals" category – people like you and me – are the ones that support nonprofit organizations. It is individuals that contribute to making many nonprofits organizations sustainable.

A common misconception in animal sheltering is that grant funding is *where it's at* for fundraising. Many small to medium-sized animal welfare groups believe they should spend the majority of their fundraising effort writing and submitting grants. Not only does the research by Giving USA (above) indicate just 15% of the total funding to all nonprofit organizations comes from foundations, but the number of national and local foundations that give specifically to animal-related causes suggest that within animal welfare, foundation support is less abundant. It is important to keep those proportions in mind as you begin developing your strategic fundraising plan.

To help illustrate the point about foundation funding in the animal welfare category, let's have you do the exercise on the next page.

Grant Makers to Animal Welfare

List as many **national** charitable foundations that fund animal welfare that you can think of:

1	
2	
3	
4	
5	
6	
7	
8	
9	
10	
11	
12	
13	
14	
15	

Based on the hundreds of workshops of workshops I've given over the years, most people are able to name 5-10 national charitable foundations that fund animal welfare. Depending on where your organization is located in the country, you may have an abundance of local foundations (like Pittsburgh, Houston or Dallas) or you may have a dearth of them (such as Detroit, Indianapolis or Milwaukee).

List of National Grant Makers to Animal Welfare

The following is a list of 15 of the most recognized national grant makers to animal welfare. (We do not list local foundations as every region of the country is different).

1	Animal Welfare Trust
2	American Humane Association (AHA)
3	Association for Protection and Cruelty of Animals (ASPCA)
4	Banfield Charitable Trust
5	Bernice Barbour Foundation
6	Build A Bear Workshop Foundation
7	Greg Biffle Foundation
8	Maddie's Fund
9	Pedigree Foundation
10	Petco Foundation
11	PetSmart Charities
12	Regina B. Frankenburg Foundation
13	Ryan Newman Foundation *(transitioning under the umbrella of Rescue Ranch)*
14	Summerlee Foundation
15	William and Charlotte Parks Foundation

Understanding Where the Money Goes To

Now that you have an understanding of where the money is coming from, let's look at where the money is going. The chart below illustrates which recipient organization categories are receiving the largest percentage of total contributions, (According *to Giving USA 2014: The Annual Report on Philanthropy for the Year 2013*):

Recipient Organization Category	Percent
Religion	31%
Education	16%
Human services	12%
Foundations	11%
Health	10%
Public-society benefit	7%
Arts, culture & humanities	5%
International Affairs	4%
Environment / Animals	3%

As you can see from the chart above, animal welfare (the last category) is in a category combined with the environment that represents just 3% (or about $10 billion) of total funding received by charitable organizations in 2013. With so much competition for donor dollars in all the categories from Religion to Education down to the Environment and Animals, it is critically important that you shift your organization from reactive or emergency-based to active and planned.

What Motivates People to Give

Let's bring your attention back to animal sheltering - specifically your organization. It is important to understand the reasons why people support your organization with a charitable contribution. By understanding motivations for giving to your organization, you can develop your fundraising activities and solicitations with those motivations in mind. List as many reasons as you can think for why people give to your organization:

1	
2	
3	
4	
5	
6	
7	
8	
9	
10	

Key Motivations for Giving

While there are many reasons, alone or in combination, that motivate a person to donate money to an animal welfare organization, I have listed the six primary reasons.

1	**Sharing Your Organization's Goals**	A person believes in your organization's mission to help pets and feels the work your organization performs makes a difference.
2	**Personal Appreciation for Your Organization**	A person is grateful to your organization for having touched them. Perhaps you helped them find their lost pet, or adopt a new pet or even vaccinated their pet(s).
3	**Joy of Giving**	Many people derive satisfaction knowing that their personal gift made, or will make, a difference for pets in your care.
4	**Being Involved**	Humans are social beings that strive to belong. Therefore, people who are passionate about pets seek out animal welfare organizations just like yours. Many people enjoy being involved whether it's helping pets through volunteering, developing long range plans by serving on the board or by funding a program or service.
5	**Being Asked**	The number one reason why a person makes a gift is because they were asked.
6	**To Help the Community**	This person may or may not even be a pet owner and they may even have little affinity for pets, yet they know that your organization fills a need that they perceive to be greatly needed in your community.

Understanding why people donate money to your organization allows you to place attention on those groups of people with a propensity to donate to your organization.

PART ONE
Message

The Need for a Case Statement

Now that you have a better understanding of where animal welfare fits into the world of charitable giving and the importance of raising *Contribution Income* to keep your nonprofit organization sustainable, we want to help you develop a strategic fundraising plan that will guide your fundraising activity. Your first step will be to develop your organization's case statement.

The case statement is the single most important document for your organization. It lays the foundation upon which all published fundraising and communication material is based from brochures to direct mail campaigns to grant submissions to newsletters and news releases.

The case statement:

- can and will persuade people to become involved with your organization
- explains why a donor's gift will make a difference to both your organization and the community
- helps maintain consistency in messaging between all of your organization's various fundraising and communication pieces

The case statement also explains:

- the need that exists
- how your organization meets/addresses that need
- reasons why a potential donor should give
- what activities a donor's gift will support
- how gifts can be made
- who supports the organization's mission
- your organization's fundraising goals
- how your organization is different from other like-mission organizations

Your organization's staff and board will use the case statement as the basis for all public messaging from fundraising and communication materials to working with members of print or broadcast media. This should result in consistent messaging.

Since the case statement is such a critical document to the organization, it should be developed with input from the board president, the executive director and input from a handful of donors (both major donors and long-term donors).

Please know and understand that developing and writing a case statement is a time consuming process that requires access to a lot of information. Please take the necessary time to get all of the information you need, and do not cut corners.

Developing Your Case Statement

The exercises on pages 32-34 and 36-39 are designed to help you assemble the various pieces of information used to develop your case statement.

You may find that many pieces of information are easy to access (such as organizational history and mission statement) and already exists elsewhere in your organization's printed or published material. This is not the time to "cut corners" and skip inclusion of that information as you develop your fundraising plan. It is important that you organize all of this material in one place, as this information is as much a part of your fundraising plan as the activities you will complete in subsequent sections of this book. Remember, anything worth doing is worth doing right.

Consider asking staff, board, volunteers, even donors for their answers to some of the other questions on the following pages, such as, "What Problem(s) Does Your Organization Address/Solve?" or "What are Your Organization's Strengths?"

By inviting others to participate in the development of your fundraising plan, you are more likely to get buy in with the final product. It is also helpful to have insight from others who have different and varying perspective on the organization. Though you may be surprised with some of the answers you receive, these answers could ultimately help your organization understand how it is perceived and how it can plan for the future.

Write a Brief Summary of Your Organization's History (2-3 paragraphs).

Write Your Organization's Mission Statement.

Write Your Organization's Mission Statement.

What Population Does Your Organization Serve? How Many Are Served?

What Problem(s) Does Your Organization Address/Solve?

What Success(es) Has Your Organization Had Addressing This/These Problem(s)?

What Are Your Organization's Primary Programs and Services?

What Would Happen to the Population You Serve if Your Organization Did Not Exist?

As you continue collecting information to develop your case statement, the next exercise on page 36 invites you to list your organization's goals. Since my experience has been that many animal sheltering organizations may not even have goals, we've included a short section about developing goals. If your organization does not have goals, this information may be beneficial to the board and executive director in developing goals for the organization. If your organization already has goals, you may want to use this information to compare what you currently have versus what is recommended here to see if your organization could benefit by adapting this system.

A Word about Developing Goals

Establishing fundraising goals is important because it helps to ensure that everyone in your organization is on the same page, working toward achieving the same results for your fundraising activities. Knowing the goals, and the tactics needed to carry out those goals, is central to meeting those goals and even adjusting strategies along the way. When developing fundraising goals for your organization it is important to use a system that clearly defines what is going to be done by spelling out specific goals rather than general ones. (*Specific Goal*: "Raise $10,000 through four direct mail campaigns by July" vs Generic Goal: "Raise more money through our direct mail program").

A system that will help you set goals and objectives are called the SMART system. SMART is an acronym that stands for:

S	Specific	What specifically do you want to accomplish?
M	Measurable	How will you measure progress? What criteria will be used?
A	Achievable	How can the goal be realistically accomplished?
R	Realistic	What history (data/stats) exists to suggest this can be achieved?
T	Time-driven	When will this be accomplished?

Examples of SMART goals:

Implement an on-line monthly giving program by September.

Increase direct mail revenue by at least 5% over last year.

Identify and submit grant proposals to three charitable foundations for the mobile adoption program by the end of Q3.

What Goals Does Your Organization Want To Accomplish?

37

How Will Your Organization Reach These Goals? (What are the Objectives?)

What Sets Your Organization Apart From Other Animal Shelters In Your Area?
(i.e. Why is Your Organization Unique? What do You Do/Offer that No One Else Does?)

What Are Your Organization's Strengths?

What Are Your Organization's Weaknesses and Challenges?

39

What Need Are You Raising Funds?

How Will Donor Funds Address The Problem(s) Identified Earlier?

What Makes Your Need Urgent?

An Animal Shelter's Guide to Fundraising
©2014 Tim Crum

Writing the Case Statement

Having completed these 15 exercises, you will reference all of this information to draft your case statement.

There are two types of case statements, an internal case statement and an external case statement. As mentioned previously, the case statement lays the foundation upon which all other fundraising and communication material is based. Therefore, the internal case statement is longer (from three to ten pages in length) and more comprehensive. It provides all details that anyone on the organization's inside (staff, board and volunteers) will need to know about your organization from history to mission to strengths to challenges to reason for seeking funds.

The external case statement draws from the internal case statement and is for a very specific audience, namely donors and prospective donors. Since this is used for external purposes, this type of case statement is typically one to two pages in length. It is both succinct and articulates everything contained in the internal case statement. Think of it as an executive summary of the internal case statement.

The internal case statement is developed first and will consume the majority of your time to develop since it will require input from other important stakeholders. (It usually goes through various revisions as it gets molded along the way). Once the internal case statement is finalized (which could take days), it is time to highlight the most important information from this document in order to create a one to two page external case statement. When finished, share the external case statement with a few select donors to ask them if the external case statement answers these questions:

- What is the need that exists?
- How do we meet/address that need?
- Why should someone support this need with a gift to us?
- What will your donor funds be used to for?
- How are we unique or different from other like-mission organizations?

Write your internal case statement using the *Internal Case Statement* form found on page 42. You will probably want to make copies of this form since the internal case statement will most likely take several pages to write.

It is very likely that this is the first time you will ever sit down to draft a case statement, internal or external. This can be a challenging process that may require several days and some help from others to complete. You may even experience writer's block. And that's OK. These things happen. What is important is taking as much time as you need to draft the internal case statement.

Although I could have included a sample of an internal and an external case statement in this book, I elected not to because when I did provide examples of case statements (in my earlier workshops), most participants had a propensity to copy the example only replacing their organization name and specific information where appropriate. Too often, I found that people were using the sample as a short cut or a "crutch". They were not developing their interpretive and writing skills, which are needed to be an effective fundraiser.

In the later workshops I gave, in which case statement examples were not provided, participants actually developed original and unique case statements. They also felt more accomplished having written a case statement, from scratch, on their own. As a result, they were more confident in their abilities and had also further developed their writing and persuasion skills.

The 64-year-old New Zealand filmmaker Lee Tamahori, best known for *Once Were Warriors* and *Die Another Day*, once said, "Always be original. Never duplicate what you've seen another actor do. Be true to the character that you've been given, and the rest will come easy."

It is with the knowledge that I challenge you to, "Be Original" as you draft your case statement. I have confidence that you **can** do this.

Internal Case Statement

Developing Your External Case Statement

Drafting your external case statement should be a much easier exercise if you completed writing the internal case statement. Remember that the external case statement is like an executive summary of the internal case statement. This document is usually one to two pages in length and is primarily used with donors and prospective donors.

Write your external case statement using the *External Case Statement* form found on the following page. You may want to make a copy of this form since the external case statement may take a second page to complete.

External Case Statement

Though you still have much work ahead of you, writing both case statements are the biggest challenges toward completing your Fundraising Plan. This is a major accomplishment and you should feel proud of what you have just completed!

Your Organization's Fundraising Past

While the case statement that you just drafted explains how your organization addresses a particular community need, a fundraising plan very specifically defines how your organization will raise funds to meet that need. Before drafting your strategic fundraising plan, you will first want to assess your organization's past fundraising efforts. After all, past fundraising efforts provides valuable insight into what has and has not worked along with clues as to why each activity may have succeeded or failed.

Fundraising History

It is important to examine your fundraising activity by category since each category uses different metrics to evaluate success of the respective fundraising activity. (We go into more detail about this subject in *Tracking and Coding Donations* on page 85.) You will group each fundraising activity into one of five categories:

1. Grants
2. Special Events
3. Direct Mail
4. On-line*
5. Other (category for all other activity that does not fall under one of the first four)

For the exercises on pages 46-50, gather as much information about your organization's fundraising activities over the past five years (using the five categories above). You will later use this information to assess past fundraising performance.

* Online fundraising is classified into two subcategories: passive and active.

Passive online fundraising are donations received through your organization's website. It's passive because you are not doing anything to solicit donations. Donations come to you. (If your organization's website does not have a "donate now" button, make sure to work with your web designer to ensure a "donate now" button is embedded into your website – preferably at the top of every page of your website).

Active online fundraising are donations received through a mass emailing to email addresses on file (similar to direct mail). Donations are actively solicited through regularly scheduled campaigns. (If your organization does not have email addresses, make sure to work with your web designer to include a "Sign Up to Receive News from Us" button embedded into your website – again, preferably at the top of every page of your website. You can also collect email addresses at your organization's front desk, on adoption applications and at community events and fairs).

GRANTS

Year	Grants Submitted	Grants Funded	Funding Amount

SPECIAL EVENTS

Year	Event Name & Type	Revenue	Expenses

DIRECT MAIL

Year	Campaign Theme & Month Sent	Revenue	Expenses

ON-LINE

Year	Campaign Theme & Month Sent	Revenue	Expenses

OTHER

Year	Activity	Revenue	Expenses

<u>Assessing Past Fundraising Activity</u>

Now that you have been able to look into the past five years of your organization's fundraising activity, it is worth examining the reasons why some fundraising activity was successful while other activity was unsuccessful. Answering these questions provides insight into which activities you should focus your time and resources on to maximize your fundraising results, as well as which activities to consider eliminating.

Let's examine metrics, by fundraising category, to understand and measure the success, or failure, of each fundraising activity:

Fundraising Category	Metrics Used
Grants	<ul><li># of grant funders identified</li><li># of grants submitted</li><li># of grants funded</li><li>% of grants funded</li><li>Reasons for grant denials</li></ul>
Special Events	<ul><li># of events</li><li># of sponsors per event</li><li># of attendees per event</li><li>Expenses for each event</li><li>Revenue for each event</li></ul>
Direct Mail	<ul><li># of campaigns</li><li>Average gift for each campaign</li><li>Response rate for each campaign</li><li>Expenses for each campaign</li><li>Revenue for each campaign</li></ul>
On-line	<ul><li># of campaigns</li><li>Average gift for each campaign</li><li>Response rate for each campaign</li><li>Open rate for each campaign</li><li>Opt outs for each campaign</li><li>Spam reports for each campaign</li><li>Expenses for each campaign</li><li>Revenue for each campaign</li></ul>
Other	?

Are there other metrics you use to evaluate the success or failure of a fundraising activity?

List those fundraising activities that were successful, metrics used and reason(s) why each campaign was successful:

SUCCESSFUL FUNDRAISING ACTIVITY

Category	Activity / Metric(s) Used	Reasons for Success
Grants		
Special Events		
Direct Mail		
On-line		
Other		

List those fundraising activities that were **<u>not</u>** successful and list the reason(s) why:

UNSUCCESSFUL FUNDRAISING ACTIVITY

Category	Activity / Metric(s) Used	Reasons Not Successful
Grants		
Special Events		
Direct Mail		
On-line		
Other		

Donors and Prospects

Let's shift our attention to all of the individuals, foundations and corporations who make up your organization's donor base.

If you recall the charitable contributions by category chart on page 22 (*Giving USA 2014: The Annual Report on Philanthropy for the Year 2013*), individuals make up the majority of donor dollars. Thus, individual donors are the livelihood of any nonprofit organization. The following exercise will help you examine the composition of your donor database, whether you track donors manually with paper files, in an Excel spreadsheet or with a donor management system.

Remember that you cannot have gifts without donors and your organization will not be successful or financially sustainable without some type of donor management system in place to track donor information and donation activity. If you currently do not have a donor management system, you need to implement one as soon as possible.

How does your organization track and manage donors? *i.e. donor management system*	
How many donors do you have in your donor management system?	

If your organization does not have a donor management system, complete this table:

How many people does your organization have mailing addresses for?	
Of the people above, how many have donated to your organization?	
How many people does your organization have e-mail addresses for?	
Of the people above, how many have donated to your organization?	
How many foundations does your organization have mailing addresses for?	
How many companies does your organization have mailing addresses for?	

Add the four shaded boxes together, this is your donor base:	

# of Individual Donations by Year (for past five years)

5 years ago	4 years ago	3 years ago	2 years ago	Last year

Change in # of Individual Donations from Year to Year for past five years

Year 5 to 4	Year 4 to 3	Year 3 to 2	Year 2 to 1

% Change in Individual Donations from Year to Year for past five years

Year 5 to 4	Year 4 to 3	Year 3 to 2	Year 2 to 1

Total # of individual donors who made the following # of gifts in the past five years:

# of Gifts Made	# of Donors
1	
2	
3-4	
5-9	
10+	

Total # of individual donors whose five year giving total fell into one of these ranges:

Total Giving	# of Donors
$ 1 -99	
$100-499	
$500-999	
$1,000-4,999	
$5,000+	

It is very important to look at these statistics since someone's past giving history is predictive of their future giving. In fact, the three most important indicators of someone's future giving are: how recently someone gave, the total number of gifts made and the total dollar amount of their giving over a five-year period.

An Animal Shelter's Guide to Fundraising
©2014 Tim Crum

Raising money from your past and current donors will not be enough to grow your funding levels, let alone maintain your current funding level. Donor acquisition (sometimes called "prospecting") is critical to the health and growth of any nonprofit organization. Each year, your organization loses donors through attrition and at the very least you should attempt to replace those lost with new donors. And if your organization is looking to increase funding, you will have to increase the total number of donors giving to your organization. Your organization will need to add more new donors than it loses from attrition.

Attrition rate

In their 2004 book, *Fundraising Management: Analysis, Planning and Practice,* authors Adrian Sargent and Elaine Jay conclude that a typical nonprofit organization will lose 50% of its donors between the first and second donation and up to 30% year over year thereafter.

On the previous page (page 55), you completed an exercise that looked at the change in the number, and percentage, of total individual donations from year to year for the past five years. In the following exercise on page 57, you will calculate your donor attrition rate, or the percent of donors who do not renew their gifts to your organization for each given year. Knowing your attrition rate impacts several other aspects of the fundraising work you do. For one, knowing your attrition rate helps you understand the number of donors you will need to acquire simply to maintain current funding levels. Two, if your attrition rate is higher than normal, it could be a sign that your organization is not perceived by those donors as being good stewards of their money. Most of the time this means one or (or sometimes both of) two things:

1. Your organization did not do a good job of thanking and acknowledging the donor for their gift.
2. Your organization is not effectively communicating with donors about what it is you are doing to fulfill your mission.

Calculating Your Attrition Rate

Insert the number of donors who gave a gift five years ago (from page 55). This is X

5 years ago

Count how many donors from five years ago, gave a gift the following year. That is Y.

4 years ago

Divide Y by X. This becomes Z.

4 / 5 years ago

Subtract Z from 100. That is A. (Express A as a percentage).

100 – Z

That is your donor attrition rate from Year 5 to Year 4.

Now calculate your donor attrition rate from years 4-3, 3-2 and 2-1.

4 years ago	3 years ago	3 / 4 years ago	100-Z	A as a %
X	Y	Z	A	

3 years ago	2 years ago	2 / 3 years ago	100-Z	A as a %
X	Y	Z	A	

2 years ago	1 year ago	1 / 2 years ago	100-Z	A as a %
X	Y	Z	A	

Unless your organization is an exception, the calculations you completed on the previous page probably show your organization losing a certain percentage of its donors each year for the past five years. If your organization is to maintain just status quo (i.e. the same number of donors from the previous year), it must replace the number of donors it lost from the previous year. If your organization wants to grow its funding levels, you need to acquire more new donors each year than you lose to offset natural attrition.

Since all nonprofit organizations lose a certain percentage of donors through natural attrition every single year, they must look toward acquiring new donors every year. The best way to acquire new donors is by targeting people who either share in your organization's goals and/or who have a personal appreciation for your organization (see **Key Motivations for Giving** on page 27).

Complete the table on page 59 to develop your first list of acquisition ("prospect") names.

Building Your Organization's First Acquisition List

Over the past five years:

How many people have adopted from your organization?	
How many people have volunteered for your organization?	
How many people have fostered pets for your organization?	
How many people have served as a board member for your organization?	
How many people have used a program or service* of your organization?	
How many people made an in-kind donation^ to your organization?	
How many companies does your organization purchase products, services or utilities from?	

Add the seven boxes together, this is your qualified prospects list:	

* *program or service could be: lost and found service, spay neuter clinic, vet services, pet food bank, etc.*

^ *Goods and/or services are donated instead of giving money to buy needed goods and services. An example of an in-kind donation is: donation of a bag of dog food, donation of a gift basket for a silent auction, donation of time from a service professional to fix the HVAC unit, etc.*

The number of qualified prospects listed on the previous page will become your first acquisition (or "prospect" list). These are the names and addresses of people that you already have access to so it makes common sense that you will solicit these people first. Since these people would appear to have a strong affinity for your organization and one or several motivating factors (i.e. personal appreciation for your organization or sharing your organizations goals), you would think that all you would have to do is ask them to make a donation and many of those people would respond with a donation right?

Well, not exactly. Here's one of the more intriguing aspects of fundraising in the animal welfare industry. Many animal sheltering professionals have found, myself included, that prospect lists comprised of adopters, volunteers, foster care providers and program/service-users typically have a lower percent response rate for solicitations than simply renting a list of qualified names. It's the case, but there are always exceptions. In fact, I worked with one humane society in northern California who mailed a solicitation to all of their pet adopters from the previous five years and they received a double digit response rate!

The only way to know if your organization is the *case* or the *exception* is to mail these lists (adopters, volunteers, foster care providers and program/service users) then track and compare the results of each list. (I include more information about coding and tracking donations later in this book (page 85).) These types of codes are referred to as "source codes" because they identify how (i.e. the source of origin) someone came into your donor management system. Using source codes makes it possible for you to understand how and which group of people (adopters, volunteers, foster care providers, etc.) performs well and where to invest your future time and resources.

Remember to create source codes to be placed on the solicitation response device that allows you to track which list donations come from, i.e. ADP for Adopters and VOL for Volunteers as some examples. This way, you can track and analyze which lists are worth an investment of your time and resources.

For comparison sake, an acceptable response rate for an acquisition campaign is between 0.5-2.5%.

PART TWO
Activity

Developing Your Fundraising Plan

Now that you've scrutinized your past fundraising activity and determined what was and was not successful, you'll want to take this knowledge to develop a calendar of fundraising activity for an entire year. A calendar of fundraising activity is a simple overview of all of the fundraising activity your organization will perform over a 12-month period. With a quick glance at this calendar, anyone can see what activity will be performed in what month. Later, you will use this simple overview to develop the budget to execute each activity.

For each fundraising category on the following page, please write down each specific fundraising activity your organization will execute by month. For example, you may list your annual *Pet Walk* under "Special Events" category for the month of May, and your *Summer Heat Campaign* under "Direct Mail" category for July. It is important to also list charitable foundations you will be applying to for grant funding since most foundations have application deadlines. (And even for those that have "open" or "rolling" applications, it is always best to plan when you will submit your grant proposal). For example, knowing that Pedigree Foundation accepts grant applications April 30 - June 30 of each year, your organization may plan to submit a grant proposal in May to help fund a Mobile Adoption Vehicle to help increase adoptions, increase awareness of adoptable pets and even serve as an emergency evacuation vehicle for at-risk animals during natural or man-made disasters. You would simply place **Pedigree Foundation: Mobile Adoption Vehicle** under the" Grants" category in the month of May.

Complete the Fundraising Activity Calendar on the following page by populating it with all of the fundraising activity your organization plans to do the following year.

Fundraising Activity Calendar

	Grants	Special Events	Direct Mail	On-line	Other
JAN					
FEB					
MAR					
APR					
MAY					
JUN					
JUL					
AUG					
SEP					
OCT					
NOV					
DEC					

Developing A Budget

With a completed outline of all fundraising activity your organization would like to execute for the following year, you will complete an exercise that assigns revenue and expenses associated with conducting these activities. As the idiom goes, "It takes money to make money." Fundraising is not free. While there are some fundraising activities that are low cost, even free, most fundraising activity will require an investment of financial and human resources. In fact, almost every successful animal sheltering organization employs a multitude of fundraising activities across the various fundraising categories, each with its own expenses. Your organization must be willing to make a financial investment in its fundraising in order to achieve a financially sustainable future. In fact, fundraising success has never been achieved without investing money into your fundraising activity.

Using the *Fundraising Activity Calendar* that you developed on the previous, you will prepare *Individual Fundraising Activity Budget* forms for each fundraising activity listed on the Calendar. An *Individual Fundraising Activity Budget* is an itemized list of the revenues and expenses associated with conducting a specific fundraising activity.

Since you will need to complete a form for every fundraising activity listed in your *Fundraising Activity Calendar*, you will want to make copies of the *Individual Fundraising Activity Budget* form found on the following page.

Some fundraising activity, such as grant submissions, may not have any associated expenses with them; therefore, you may decide not to complete an *Individual Fundraising Budget* for grants.

65

Individual Fundraising Activity Budget

ACTIVITY	
DATE OF ACTIVITY	
ACTIVITY MANAGED BY	

ACTIVITY REVENUE AND EXPENSES

ITEMIZED REVENUE	$	ITEMIZED EXPENSES	$
TOTAL REVENUE	$	**TOTAL EXPENSES**	$
ACTIVITY NET TOTAL= **TOTAL REVENUE – TOTAL EXPENSES**			$

Fundraising Budget

Now that you have completed an *Individual Fundraising Budget* form for each of your organization's fundraising activities, it is time to compile all of this information into one master budget for your organization's fundraising program. Your overall budget usually becomes one of the ways in which you will measure the performance of the entire fundraising program.

FUNDRAISING BUDGET			

FUNDRAISING REVENUE		FUNDRAISING EXPENSES	
Grants	$	Grants	$
Special Events		Special Events	
Direct Mail		Direct Mail	
On-line		On-line	
Other		Other	
TOTAL REVENUE	$	TOTAL EXPENSES	$
FUNDRAISING NET TOTAL= FUNDRAISING REVENUE – FUNDRAISING EXPENSES			$

Building a Timeline for Fundraising Activity

As you can probably see from the Fundraising Activity Calendar on page 63, your organization has a variety of fundraising activities across each of the fundraising categories: Grants, Special Events, Direct Mail, On-line campaigns and even Other activities. Keeping track of each of these activities and the myriad of responsibilities that go along with each one can be a challenging assignment. And the more fundraising activities that are planned, the more tasks that will overlap. When tasks overlap, there is a good chance that some tasks may be accidentally forgotten or missed – especially if you are a one-person fundraising department.

To keep all of these activities and tasks organized, you will complete an *Individual Fundraising Activity Timeline.* The Timeline is a comprehensive list specifying every task that needs to be performed along the way toward carrying out a fundraising activity.

In addition to maintaining organization for your fundraising activity there is another very important reason for completing these *Individual Fundraising Activity Timelines.* Oftentimes in animal welfare, one person will maintain control over a particular event. This person may know every task that needs to be completed; they may know every person that needs to be contacted, every email address and phone number, deadlines, etc. However, if this person were to leave (voluntarily or involuntarily), they take with them knowledge about that fundraising activity – knowledge that could hinder the organization's ability to successfully carry out the event. Remember, fundraising activities are really the property of the organization, not the individual who manages it.

Yet another reason to complete the *Individual Fundraising Activity Timelines* is the ability to make future fundraising planning much easier and smoother. For example, if your organization does an annual Pet Walk this year on October 11th, it is very likely that very event will be held around the same day the following year. If you have taken the time to list every task in the *Individual Fundraising Activity Timeline* this year, then next year's Timeline will probably just require an adjustment of the dates in the timeline.

Completing an *Individual Fundraising Activity Timeline* is the most time intensive and laborious part of putting together your fundraising plan. Some activities, particularly those falling under the Special Events category, may have a timeline that run several pages long. In fact, I planned a Pet Walk for one organization that had a timeline of 17-pages – and that was just for one event!

Based on reaction from my direct reports, those whom I tasked with putting together *Individual Fundraising Activity Timelines*, were none too happy. The *Timelines* were time and labor intensive. Yet, when the *Timelines* were complete and the event came around next year, those very staff members usually thanked me for having them take the time and effort to put the *Timeline* together.

Going into this next task, you know it will require time to put it together, so please take the necessary time to write down every task that needs to be completed for each activity. Since you will need to complete an *Individual Fundraising Activity Timeline* for every fundraising activity listed in your *Fundraising Activity Calendar*, you may first want to make copies of the *Individual Fundraising Activity Timeline* forms found on the next two pages. You will make only one copy of Page 69 for each fundraising activity since it is the "title" page. However, multiple copies of page 70 may be made for each fundraising activity depending on the number of tasks that need to be completed.

How to complete an Individual Fundraising Activity Timeline
The *Individual Fundraising Activity Timeline* is like a road map that takes you from the start of the event to the finish. It is important to prepare this in chronological order of tasks to be completed starting with the first task all the way through to the last task (many tasks occur after the fundraising event is done). As you begin this exercise, notice that the *Individual Fundraising Activity Timeline* has many rows, each containing the following headers: Task, Task Due By, Person Responsible and Notes.

The **Task** is an assignment for someone to complete, for example:
"Complete paperwork for parade permit with City Parks & Recreation Department"

Task Due By is the expected date of completion of the assignment, for example:
"May 12, 2015"

Person Responsible is the name of the individual who is responsible for completing this particular assignment. This helps reduce confusion and missed assignments since the person responsible for each task is defined during the planning stage. For example: *"Rebecca Brody"*

The **Notes** section contains any information that is helpful in the completion of the task. This may consist of contact names, email addresses, phone numbers, websites and costs. For example,
"Dir. of Parks & Rec is Rick Wilson. rwilson@city.prdept.gov. 412.555.1234."

Using the information from the examples above, one row of information from your *Individual Fundraising Activity Timeline* may look like this:

Task	Task Due By	Person Responsible	Notes
Complete paperwork for parade permit with City Parks & Rec. Dept.	*May 12,2015*	*Rebecca Brody*	*Rick Wilson. Dir of Parks & Rec rwilson@city.prdept.gov. 412.555.1234*

Individual Fundraising Activity Timeline

ACTIVITY	

DATE OF ACTIVITY	

ACTIVITY MANAGED BY	

Task	Task Due By	Person Responsible	Notes

Task	Task Due By	Person Responsible	Notes

PART THREE
Goals

> ## *"If it's worth doing, it's worth measuring."*

Establishing Goals

On page 35, we shared with you the importance of establishing fundraising goals and on page 36 you completed an exercise in which you listed the goals for your organization. Hopefully one of those organizational goals related to the fundraising efforts of your organization. (In fact, a best practice is for your organization to have one goal related to each area of the organization, i.e. adoptions, staffing, fundraising, volunteering, marketing, medical care, etc.). Since you are creating a fundraising plan for your organization, all of the fundraising activities you have been working on in the preceding pages (pages 63, 65, 66, 69, 70) should ultimately work toward achieving the overall fundraising goal. (Most likely, the internal case statement that you developed earlier included the organization's overall fundraising goal). Even if your organization does not have organizational goals, it is important for you to establish an overall goal for your fundraising efforts so you have a way of determining where you are headed.

The following exercise requires you to create one to three goals for each of the fundraising activities you have listed in the *Fundraising Activity Calendar* (page 63). These goals become the guiding light for that specific activity and will be used in determining the success or failure of that fundraising activity.

For example, you may establish the three following goals for your March 2015 direct mail campaign:

GOALS
1   Generate a net income of $2,000
2   Have a minimum response rate of 6.5%
3   Have an average gift of at least $22.00

These three goals, if met, define success for this activity.

Using the *Fundraising Activity Goals* form on the following page, please list one to three goals for each of the fundraising activities that your organization will conduct. You may want to make copies of the *Fundraising Activity Goals* form found on the following page.

<u>Fundraising Activity Goals</u>

Category: Grants	Fundraising Activity	Goals
		1.
		2.
		3.
		1.
		2.
		3.
		1.
		2.
		3.
		1.
		2.
		3.
		1.
		2.
		3.
		1.
		2.
		3.

An Animal Shelter's Guide to Fundraising
©2014 Tim Crum

Fundraising Activity Goals

Category: Special Events	Fundraising Activity	Goals
		1.
		2.
		3.
		1.
		2.
		3.
		1.
		2.
		3.
		1.
		2.
		3.
		1.
		2.
		3.
		1.
		2.
		3.

Fundraising Activity Goals

Category: Direct Mail	Fundraising Activity	Goals
		1.
		2.
		3.
		1.
		2.
		3.
		1.
		2.
		3.
		1.
		2.
		3.
		1.
		2.
		3.
		1.
		2.
		3.

<u>Fundraising Activity Goals</u>

Category: On-line	Fundraising Activity	Goals
		1.
		2.
		3.
		1.
		2.
		3.
		1.
		2.
		3.
		1.
		2.
		3.
		1.
		2.
		3.
		1.
		2.
		3.

Fundraising Activity Goals

Category: Other	Fundraising Activity	Goals
		1.
		2.
		3.
		1.
		2.
		3.
		1.
		2.
		3.
		1.
		2.
		3.
		1.
		2.
		3.
		1.
		2.
		3.

Supporting Your Fundraising Activity

Fundraising does not work in a vacuum. Just because you take the time to put together a comprehensive fundraising plan, then spend the time executing all of the various tasks, does not automatically mean you will be successful. Even though people are motivated to make a donation to an organization for a variety of reasons (see page 27), two things must exist before those motivations even kick in:

1. A person, company or foundation must know your organization (after all, who gives to an organization they have never heard of?)
2. A person, company or foundation must feel good about your organization (rare is the case when someone makes a donation to an organization they do not feel good about)

This requires an accompanying plan to increase the awareness and reputation of your organization in addition to your plan to raise money. To this end, you will want to develop a plan that places your organization on a steady diet of news releases designed to generate news, and therefore, awareness, of your organization. (We recommend distribution of a news release every two weeks). This is best achieved through the distribution of news releases (and not just on your organization's Facebook page since your Facebook page typically reaches an audience of people who already know and support your organization).

We recommend using a news wire service to distribute your news releases. A news wire service delivers your news release to their network of journalists and news Web sites. Many services will also index your news release on major search engines (like Google, and Yahoo) allowing anyone searching for news about your organization a greater chance of finding your news release online. There are numerous news release services that exist, each with various benefits and costs, so it will be up to you to compare the cost vs benefit to decide which news wire service is best for you. Best practice is to use a combination of both paid and free news wire distribution services as each has unique benefits. Here is a short list of some paid and free news wire distribution services (though there are far more than listed here):

Paid:	PR Newswire	PR Web	PR Hwy
Free:	PR Urgent	PR Log	Newsvine

Your best approach is to plan out the news releases you intend to issue throughout the year. This will provide your organization with some structure to adhere to and helps you stay focused on your goal of continually generating news about your organization. Although you will have to remain flexible as some news stories just happen organically and cannot be planned for in advance.

Believe it or not, there are already a good number of news events that you can plan for in advance. The first place for you to look is the *Fundraising Activity Calendar* that you developed (page 63). Many of the activities that fall under the Special Events category could result in the issuance of a news release, as well as any grant funds awarded to your organization.

The second place to look for news ideas are the special days, weeks and months that are held throughout the year in support of pets. These events are typically sponsored by a national organization. Many of these events include activities and a press kit for your organization to use. These special days, weeks and months represent an opportunity for your organization to generate news, and therefore awareness, about your organization. For more information about these special days, weeks and months, visit the website of the sponsor.

Here are just some of the special days

Month	Event	Sponsor
January	National Train Your Dog Month	Association of Professional Dog Trainers
February	Spay/Neuter Awareness Month	HSUS
	World Spay Day	Humane Society International
March	National Puppy Day	None
April	Prevention of Cruelty to Animals Month	ASPCA
	Free Feral Cat Spay Day	Alley Cat Rescue
May	Be Kind to Animals Week	American Humane Association
June	Just One Day	No Kill Advocacy Center
	Adopt-a-Shelter-Cat Month	ASPCA
July	National Craft for Your Local Shelter Day	None
August	International Homeless Animals Day	Int'l Society for Animal Rights
September	Adopt-a-Less-Adoptable-Pet Week	Petfinder.com
October	Adopt-a-Shelter-Cat Month	American Humane Association
November	National Animal Shelter Appreciation Week	HSUS
December	National Mutt's Day	Colleen Paige OmniMedia

Using a mix of your own fundraising activities combined with the special days listed above, you can complete the *Calendar of News Release Activity* on the following page by populating it with some stories your organization will distribute to news outlets. (*Fundraising Activity Calendar* page 63). You will still need to generate additional news releases since it is best to distribute a news release every two weeks (or a minimum of 24 per year).

Be mindful of other stories that are happening in your organization. (A good idea is to stay in close contact with those in your animal intake and/or veterinary medical department. Ask them to let you know – immediately – of any unusual stories or cases. This will allow you to gain information and take photos as the story happens. You will probably discover many interesting and unusual newsworthy stories happening around your shelter every day).

Calendar of News Release Activity

	JAN	FEB	MAR	APR	MAY	JUN	JUL	AUG	SEP	OCT	NOV	DEC
News Release												

Finalizing Your Fundraising Plan

You are almost done with your fundraising plan. Since you have been very busy assembling all of the various parts of your fundraising plan, it's now time to compile all of these parts into one final ***draft*** form for distribution to your organization's leadership (executive director, board of directors) for final approval. If during the drafting process of this fundraising plan you were able to collaborate and incorporate ideas from others (especially those with authority to approve the plan) it is more likely to be accepted with little, if any, opposition. Be prepared, however, to justify each individual fundraising activity using historical fundraising performance and other supporting data and/or facts. The approving body will most likely want to understand the reasons and financial impact an activity has on the organization's overall fundraising efforts when approving.

To assist you with assembling a cohesive and flowing fundraising plan, I've included a sample outline that illustrates the order of material for your final draft. You can simply take all of your completed exercises and assemble them in one document or you may want to consider typing all of your completed exercises into a Microsoft Word file. Section IV of your fundraising plan are documents important to your organization's fundraising. We cover these documents on pages 93-96.

ORGANIZATION NAME
STRATEGIC FUNDRAISING PLAN

SECTION I. ORGANIZATION
History
Mission (and Vision)

SECTION II. FUNDRAISING BACKGROUND
of Donors
Attrition Rate
Five Year Fundraising History

SECTION III. ACTIVITY
Fundraising Budget
Fundraising Activity Calendar
Individual Fundraising Activity Budget
Individual Fundraising Activity Timelines
Fundraising Activity Goals
Calendar of News Release Activity

SECTION IV. FUNDRAISING DOCUMENTS
Board Giving Policy
Donor Bill of Rights
Donor Privacy Policy
Gift Acceptance Policy

Once you put all of the components of your strategic fundraising plan together using the outline on the previous page, it's time to submit it for approval. When it has been officially approved, you should make copies and distribute the approved plan to all members of the board, executive director (and other director-level staff) along with anyone else with a responsibility to raise funds. Your fundraising plan is now your road map leading to fundraising success.

It is important to constantly monitor the fundraising plan and all of its activity. The board may want to receive status updates about the plan's progress at every board meeting. They may look at things such as actual figures versus budgeted numbers. This can help them work with the organization's executive director in order to allocate any financial and human resources needed to help with executing the plan.

Staff and volunteers would even benefit by receiving regular reports about fundraising activity. (We suggest preparing and distributing reports to staff and volunteers on a monthly basis). This helps others begin to understand the critical role that fundraising plays in the overall operations of your organization and may even lead to others becoming more involved with your fundraising efforts.

The following pages (pages 83-92) cover important topics related to fundraising. It is imperative that you become familiar with these five issues since all of them impact your fundraising efforts.

The majority of this book is devoted to putting together a plan to solicit donations. Yet, fundraising is more than having a plan and asking for money. It is equally as much about thanking your donors for their gifts. You see, simply expressing your appreciation in a timely manner is one of the keys to retaining your donors.

If you recall from earlier in the book (page 56), a typical nonprofit organization will lose 50% of its donors between the first and second donation and up to 30% year over year thereafter. You even completed some exercises to determine the attrition rate for your own organization. If you discovered that your organization's attrition rate is higher than a typical nonprofit organization, it could mean that your organization was not doing a good job of thanking and acknowledging donors for their gift. Though this next section is brief, its importance to your overall fundraising effort is significant.

Thank you Letters
Thanking someone for making a donation to your organization may not seem like a big deal to you, yet it remain one of the best tools you have at your disposal to cultivate a long-term relationship with a donor. A thank you actually does several very important things. A thank you:
1. acknowledges to the donor that you received their donation
2. connects the donors' gift back to their original motivation for giving
3. provides another opportunity to communicate with the donor
4. reinforces your organization's name with the donor
5. demonstrates responsible handling of their funds
6. can serve as documented proof for the donor's tax purposes* (see page 84)

Timely and meaningful gift acknowledgments are essential to donor satisfaction and retention. Therefore, it is critical that your organization make every effort to have a quick turnaround for acknowledgement of gifts. Industry best practice is to send a donor's "thank you" for their gift within 72 hours after your organization received it. Even the Donor's Bill of Rights (see #5 under Donor's Bill of Rights on page 94) identifies appropriate acknowledgement as among a donor's rights.

Your acknowledgement provides positive reinforcement to the donor that they made a good decision to support your organization. It also sends a subtle message to the donor that your organization is organized and engages in good business practices – and that builds donor's confidence in your organization. You will find that simply thanking donors for their gift is one of the best things you can do.

I'd like to share a personal story to demonstrate how impactful a thank you letter can be to a donor.

Several years ago, as executive director of a large humane society, I had met one of the organization's donors at one of the humane society events. Svetlana was an elderly woman who shared with me about her childhood growing up in Leningrad (Russia), known as St. Petersburg since 1991.

I listened intently as Svetlana shared many fascinating stories about her upbringing, family and her life in Russia. It was a treat for me to hear her stories.

As executive director, I would sign all acknowledgement letters for gifts of $500 or more. Many months after the event, Svetlana had made a large donation to the humane society and her acknowledgement letter came across my desk for me to sign.   (When I signed letters I also like to include a personal note to the donor if I knew something about them such as asking about their pets, kids or business). Knowing that Svetlana still spoke and read Russian, I wrote a personal note to her entirely in Russian using the Cyrillic alphabet. (I had studied and learned Russian during my college years).

When she received the acknowledgement letter, Svetlana was deeply touched that I had written in her native language and remembered enough about her to include a personal message to her based on our conversation months earlier. To this very day, when someone from the humane society talks with Svetlana, she always mentions that thank you letter I wrote to her. That speaks to the power of a thank you letter.

* Although a donor must have a written record for any donation they make in order to deduct the amount from their tax return, regardless of the amount, IRS rules require an individual or corporation that makes a donation of $250 or more looking to claim a deduction, obtain a donation receipt with three declarations:
    1. A statement that the charity received the contribution
    2. The amount of the contribution or a description of the property contributed
    3. A statement whether the donor received any goods or services in exchange for the contribution

For more information about this topic, we recommend visiting the IRS website at www.irs.gov and reviewing:

IRS Publication 526. Charitable Contributions
This publication explains how to claim a deduction for charitable contributions. It discusses organizations qualified to receive them, the types of contributions you can deduct, how much you can deduct, what records to keep, and how to report them.

IRS Publication. Determining the Value of Donated Property
This publication is designed to help donors and appraisers determine the value of property (other than cash) that is given to qualified organizations. It also explains what kind of information you must have to support the charitable contribution deduction you claim on your return.

You may also want to consult with a tax accountant or a tax attorney.

Tracking and Coding Donations

Donors and donations are the lifeblood of any nonprofit organization so it's important for your organization to always focus on tracking and recording each gift. As stated earlier (page 45), your organization's past fundraising efforts provide valuable insight into what has and has not worked, which can only be gauged if your organization kept records about its fundraising activity. (Not only does the donation history help your organization track and monitor fundraising activity, but as a nonprofit organization you must keep accurate donation records so that you can provide donors with donation receipts for tax purposes). The more information that was recorded about donations, the more valuable the data becomes.

If your organization has not kept accurate donation records, whether in a donor management system or manually, here are the pieces of information about a donation you will want to track and monitor.

Who Gave	The name(s) and complete contact information of the individual(s), company or foundation that made a donation
What they Gave	The dollar amount of the gift (or grant) along with how the gift was made (cash, check, credit card, stock, etc.)
When they Gave	The date of the donation
Where they Gave	Was this a gift to the general fund (i.e. operations, annual fund) or was the gift restricted* to a particular program or service (i.e. low cost spay/neuter clinic)
Why they Gave^	What prompted the donor to make the donation (i.e. direct mail campaign, on-line solicitation, website, PetWalk)

* see page 89 for more information about restricted vs unrestricted gifts

^ Why someone gave to your organization is critical to document since most gifts to your organization are stimulated by a specific fundraising activity. You will need to track and monitor the origins of each donation so that you can make decisions about future fundraising activity based on what is, and isn't, working.

For example, your organization may produce four direct mail campaigns each year. In order to track which of those four campaigns is receiving which donations, your organization will want to place a different code on each campaign's pledge card. This way, every time a pledge card is received, your organization can look at the code to determine what campaign was the source of the donation. A simple yet highly effective coding system includes a five-letter acronym to represent the fundraising activity followed by a three-letter month and two number year of the campaign. In the following sample, DMAILSEP14 is the code for Direct Mail Campaign sent in September 2014. Each pledge card returned with a donation bearing the code (DMAILSEP14) will be credited to that specific fundraising activity. Here is what the codes for the four direct mail campaigns that your organization produces for the year could look like: DMAILMAR14, DMAILMAY14, DMAILSEP14, and DMAILDEC14

Codes are not limited to just direct mail. Every fundraising activity in each of the five categories, would receive a code. The following are just some examples of codes:

PWALKOCT14	Code for your organization's PetWalk held in October 2014
BLTIEFEB09	Code for the Black Tie Dinner event your organization held back in February 2009, while BLTIEFEB10 would be the code for the same event held the following year in 2010. Codes for this event in subsequent years would look like: BLTIEFEB11, BLTIEFEB12, BLTIEFEB13, BLTIEFEB14, etc.

But not every donation your organization receives in the mail comes with a pledge card or some other way of tracking its original fundraising activity. In fact, sometimes individuals and/or companies make unsolicited donations to your organization. We refer to these as "white mail" and code them as such. (White mail gets its name from the plain "white" envelope the donation arrives in, although the envelope could really be any color). If you receive a donation in the mail that comes without any type of pledge card or lacking any type of return envelope provided by your organization, then these donations should be recorded as white mail for that month. The code is usually WMAIL followed by a three-letter month and two number year of when the donation was received. WMAILAUG14 are those unsolicited donations that arrived in August 2014, while WMAILSEP14 are those unsolicited donations that arrived in the following month, September 2014. By coding and tracking, you may soon discover trends to your fundraising activity. But you can only do this if you code and track donations!

Whether you record donation activity with a donor management system or manually using hard copy records, you will want to capture three things about all donations:

1. **Donor Contact Information**
2. **Donation Specifics** (*We covered what information you should record about donation specifics on the previous page*)
3. **Donor Notes**

Donor Contact Information

When possible, request, or attempt to gather, the following information from each donor:

- First and Last Name (include prefixes and/or suffixes, i.e. Dr. , Jr., III)
- Complete mailing address
- City, State, and ZIP code (each in its own separate field)
- Telephone numbers (Home, Work, Mobile – again each with its own separate field)
- E-mail address
- Spouse, significant other and children (each in its own separate field)

Donor Notes

Not only are donors the lifeblood of your organization, they are also the individuals, companies and foundations who have engaged in a relationship with your organization. As with any relationship in life, they work best when both sides are committed to the other. (Sadly, far too many animal sheltering organizations simply view donors as dollar symbols to help them. It's time to change that thinking). The more you know about your donors, the more opportunities you have to reinforce the relationship your organization has with them.

Keeping notes about your donors shifts the focus from viewing donors merely as money providers to viewing them as equal participants in a relationship with your organization. You will want to pay attention to any information about your donors so that you can record the information in the notes section of their donor files. You will record things such as:

- Names, breeds, and ages of their pets
- Names and ages of their children
- Employer and job title
- Volunteer activity
- Attendance at events
- Any life changes (marriage, birth of child, new job, graduation from college, death of family member, awards or achievements)
- Along with any written notes received from the donor

As you enter donor notes, it is critical to have a system in place to review this information any time the donor makes a gift or the organization expects to interact with the donor (such as at an event). The information in the donor notes field can be recalled when communicating and/or interacting with the donor. Your donors will greatly appreciate that you recalled their cat's names, or the fact their daughter "Sophia" just graduated from high school, or that their favorite hockey team just won the Stanley Cup. This information can be used in a personal conversation with the donor or when writing a personal note on a thank you letter to the donor for their recent $50 gift.

Remember that donors are engaged in a relationship with your organization. It is your organization's responsibility to further cultivate these relationships. After all, future giving depends, in part, on how well you've nurtured the donor's relationship with your organization. If you recall from page 56, a typical nonprofit organization will lose 50% of its donors between the first and second donation. You can help your organization retain a higher percentage off its donations by cultivating relationships with your donors.

Restricted vs Unrestricted Gifts

Donations that your organization receives are classified as one of two types of gifts: restricted or unrestricted. It is critical that you understand the difference between these two types of gifts as there are specific financial management obligations with restricted gifts.

Unrestricted donations are donations received by your organization that are free from any external restrictions and usually go toward the operating expenses of the organization or allocated for whatever purpose deemed appropriate by the organization. Most individual contributions are unrestricted, as are general operating and unrestricted grants.

Restricted donations are contributions received by your organization in which the donor restricts funding to be used for a specific purpose or for a specific period of time. Often times, grant funding is designated for a specific purpose, such as providing spay/neuter surgery to pets of residents with low income. Organizations should exercise caution when establishing restricted funds since there is a risk that the organization can raise more money for a specific purpose than is actually needed. In these cases the organization is ethically and legally obligated to use funds for their designated purpose. If an organization does not use restricted funds as intended, the donor can request full return of their donation, pursue legal action, or even file a complaint with your State's Office of the Attorney General. Any of these actions can be very damaging to your organization's reputation. It will also have a major impact on future donations to your organization. Therefore, it is best to fully understand your obligations

We highly recommend that you consult with a tax accountant regarding your organization's restricted funds. You will want to ensure that any restricted funds are accurately recorded and accounted for in all financial accounts and reports. You may also want to contact an attorney specializing in nonprofit law to review the setup of your organization's restricted funds. They can review the language of each restricted fund to make certain the fundraising material is not too restrictive. For example, many restricted funds will include a clause similar to this,

"Any funds raised above and beyond what is needed for the purpose of the XYZ Fund, may be used for other purposes as deemed appropriate by [organization name]." *

* The example above does not constitute legal advice.

Legal and Ethical Considerations

It is imperative that you know and comply with registration requirements for your organization to solicit contributions in states with such requirements. Failure to register in a state where you are required to is illegal and may result in fines and in some cases your organization can be penalized by having to cease any type of solicitations in that state. In the past few years, the IRS and state governments have been cracking down on nonprofit organizations who fail to register in states with specific solicitation registration requirements. Needless to say, the damage to your organization's reputation and fundraising activity from a fine or penalty can be catastrophic.

All states other than the 11 identified below require nonprofits that solicit contributions from state residents to register with a state agency.

Arizona	Iowa	Texas
Delaware	Montana	Vermont
Idaho	Nebraska	Wyoming
Indiana	South Dakota	

Solicitations can include any type of requests for donations whether the request is made by mail, phone, email, on-line (Internet) or by advertisement. Even if your organization does not receive any donations from the solicitation activity, your organization is still required to register.

In a move to get nonprofit organizations to comply with state registration requirements, the IRS recently revised Form 990 to now require nonprofit organizations to provide information about their state registration.

Since each state has different requirements, your nonprofit organization must individually register with each state where it is required to do so. The more states your organization fundraises in, the more states where you may have to register. Even the name for registration varies by state. Some states refer to it simply as a registration statement, while others may refer to it as a license, certificate or solicitation permit.

You should also be aware that some states even have requirements for professional fundraising companies that conduct fundraising activity on behalf of your organization. If you outsource some or all of your organization's fundraising, ask your fundraising consultant if they are in compliance with your state requirements.

To learn more about state registration requirements for nonprofits visit the website of the *National Association of State Charity Officials*.

The Board's Role in Fundraising

A board member is a fiduciary under the law and is responsible for the stewardship of a nonprofit organization and ensuring that the organization is fulfilling its mission. Responsibilities of board members fall into one of four categories:

F	Financial	Develop, approve and monitor the budget Ensure adequate financial resources Protect assets and provide proper financial oversight
R	Reputation	Enhance the organization's public image
O	Oversight	Select the executive Support the executive Review the performance of the executive
G	Governance	Determine the organization's mission and purpose Develop and monitor the organization's long term plans Establish and assess the organization's programs and services

As you can see from the list of responsibilities above, board members are not only charged with how the organization's funds are managed and spent, but also with the acquisition and availability of money, which involves fundraising. This means board members are fundamentally involved in raising money for your nonprofit organization. The best way for a board member to demonstrate his or her commitment as a fundraiser is to make a cash donation to the organization (every year), regardless of their own personal financial situation or how much time they donate.

Board members who support their own organization with a cash contribution provide credibility to the board and to the organization. After all, why should anyone else provide financial support to your organization if the very people entrusted with its financial stewardship are not? Your organization becomes credible, and asking becomes easier, when board members have demonstrated their own financial commitment to the organization. Since the board is responsible for providing a sound financial foundation for the organization, personal contributions demonstrate their commitment to this responsibility as well as their confidence that the organization is handling contributions in an appropriate manner.

An Animal Shelter's Guide to Fundraising
©2014 Tim Crum

Board members have four responsibilities related to fundraising for the organization:

1   To make a financial contribution to the extent of their capacity. This is usually addressed by a board giving policy (see page 93). Bear in mind that many funders, particularly foundations and major donors, will ask if 100% of your board members make a financial contribution to the organization.

2   To solicit contributions from people in their network. Remember that the number one reason why a person makes a gift to your organization is because they are asked (and usually asked by the right person).

3   To help recruit new board members who have affluence or influence in order to ensure the success of your organization's fundraising endeavors. Most successful nonprofit boards contain at least a few affluent people who have the ability to make generous donations and who also have the ability to utilize their network of affluent and influential people to support your organization.

4   To oversee your organization's fundraising efforts. Board members are responsible for making sure that your organization is pursuing funds by every appropriate means, which includes development and execution of a written fundraising plan.

Board Giving Policy

A board giving policy is introduced and approved by the governing body requiring board members to give money – in addition to time and expertise – to the organization for which they serve. The amount of giving required by a board giving policy varies from place to place depending on variables from local economy to organizational age to reputation to prestige. It is important for the board to discuss an appropriate amount for the policy as a high dollar amount may serve to exclude quality members who cannot afford the amount whereas a low dollar amount may actually leave money on the table as wealthier board members may give precisely the amount in the policy despite having a capacity to give far greater than what the policy calls for.

There are several ways for a board to structure its board giving policy:

- Establish a minimal amount but encourage donations above and beyond the minimum for those who have greater capacity.

- Create a range for giving with a set minimum and maximum.

- Implement a policy based on an individual board member's own financial means.

- Establish a "get or give"-type policy allowing for each member to raise the funds or make a personal gift, or some combination of both.

Whatever type of policy is used, it is critical for your board to have an established and formal board giving policy that articulates each board member's financial commitment to the organization.

A Donor Bill of Rights

The Donor Bill of Rights was created in 1993 by the National Society of Fundraising Executives (NSFRE), American Association of Fundraising Council (AAFRC), the Association for Healthcare Professionals (AHP), and the Council for Advancement and Support of Education (CASE). The Bill lends support to ethical practices, accountability and disclosure to ensure donor awareness of a charity's fundraising activity and responsibilities.

Philanthropy is based on voluntary action for the common good. It is a tradition of giving and sharing that is primary to the quality of life. To ensure that philanthropy merits the respect and trust of the general public, and that donors and prospective donors can have full confidence in the not-for-profit organizations and causes they are asked to support, we declare that all donors have these rights:

1. To be informed of the organization's mission, of the way the organization intends to use donated resources, and of its capacity to use donations effectively for their intended purposes.
2. To be informed of the identity of those serving on the organization's governing board, and to expect the board to exercise prudent judgment in its stewardship responsibilities.
3. To have access to the organization's most recent financial statements.
4. To be assured their gifts will be used for the purposes for which they were given.
5. To receive appropriate acknowledgement and recognition.
6. To be assured that information about their donations is handled with respect and with confidentiality to the extent provided by law.
7. To expect that all relationships with individuals representing organizations of interest to the donor will be professional in nature.
8. To be informed whether those seeking donations are volunteers, employees of the organization or hired solicitors.
9. To have the opportunity for their names to be deleted from mailing lists that an organization may intend to share.
10. To feel free to ask questions when making a donation and to receive prompt, truthful and forthright answers.

Donor Privacy Policy

Through the years, donors have conveyed concern regarding the use of their personal information by nonprofit organizations. Most donors expect their information to be kept confidential and even seek assurances regarding the privacy and protection of their personal information. This has resulted in many nonprofit organizations publishing a donor privacy policy which articulates how the organization handles personal information about its donors.

The following is a sample of a donor privacy policy:

XYZ organization *does not sell, trade or otherwise share a donor's personal information with anyone at any time (other than to process donations).*

However, if your organization does sell, trade or share donor information with other entities, it is critical that you publish how donors can have their name and contact information removed from such lists.

It is best practice for your organization to have a privacy policy and ensure that it is published on your organization's website.

Gift Acceptance Policy

While most nonprofit organizations are generally grateful for any donations, there are actually some kinds of gifts that your organization just may not be prepared to accept or that may not be worth the time, energy and expense to accept. For example, is your organization prepared to accept the donation of someone's vehicle? What if that vehicle was severely rusted with no tires and was sitting on cinder blocks in a wooded lot?

Those questions are best left answered by your organization's gift acceptance policy. A gift acceptance policy clearly defines your organization's position on non-cash gifts and what you will, and won't accept. This helps to eliminate the struggle with a staff person trying to decide whether to accept or deny a gift because the policy defines that for you.

A gift acceptance policy is a policy that the board enacts. This takes the individual decision-making process off of staff and onto the board, where it belongs. Once a gift acceptance policy is passed by the board, the policy should be published on your website. This helps the organization manage donor's expectations and can be used as a reference point for donors when they want to give your organization something akin to the "rusted vehicle with no tires sitting on cinder blocks in a wooded lot".

Note: The redesigned 990 asks on Schedule M whether a nonprofit has a "gift acceptance policy" that requires the review of any "non-standard gifts" (gifts other than cash or check).

Congratulations

You did it!

You developed your own fundraising plan.

You should feel proud of your accomplishment.

Permissions and Sources

Page	Source
Front Cover	Front cover images from: ©Bigstockphoto.com/ehammer ©Bigstockphoto.com/jagodka ©Bigstockphoto.com/kurhan ©Fotolia.com/scottchan ©iStock.com/fotojagodka
17	http://www.aspca.org/about-us/faq/pet-statistics ASPCA National Council on Pet Population Study and Policy Ralston Purina
21	http://www.irs.gov http://www.irs.gov/pub/irs-pdf/p1771.pdf http://www.irs.gov/publications/p526/
22	Giving USA Reprinted with permission.
25	Giving USA. Reprinted with permission.
56	*Fundraising Management: Analysis, Planning and Practice* by Adrian Sargeant and Elaine Joy. 2004. Routledge. London, England. Reprinted with permission.
84	http://www.irs.gov http://www.irs.gov/publications/p526/ http://www.irs.gov/publications/p561/ Internal Revue Service
97	Page images from: ©Dollarphotoclub/peterfactors ©Bigstockphoto.com/jagodka
Back Cover	Back cover images from: ©Fotolia.com/arcady ©Fotolia.com/scottchan ©iStock.com/fotojagodka

About the Author

Tim Crum is a nationally recognized expert on fundraising in the animal welfare industry who is often called upon to speak at national and regional conferences. As founder and CEO of Animal Shelter Fundraising, Tim has consulted with more than 100 animal welfare groups across the country since the company's inception in 2008. He has raised in excess of $200,000,000 for both local and national animal welfare groups during his career. In addition to his fundraising work, he has visited and toured 300+ animal shelters in 49 states (North Dakota is the exception) and seven countries.

Tim is also the lead presenter for Humane College. He travels extensively around the country giving fundraising workshops, presentations and motivational speeches to hundreds of animal welfare professionals each year. His fundraising knowledge, coupled with his creativity, enthusiasm and quick wit make him popular with audiences.

A native of Pennsylvania, Tim has worked in fundraising for his entire 27-year professional career. During this time, Tim has been the executive director of two animal shelters; director of one government-run animal care and control agency; and development director for one animal shelter. As director of development and marketing for PetSmart Charities he transformed the organization from $10M in annual contributions to over $30M in just four years.

Tim graduated from the University of Pittsburgh with a Bachelor of Arts degree and completed 20-credits towards a Master's Degree from the University of Pittsburgh's Graduate School of Public and International Affairs.

Tim is married with two children and resides in suburban Phoenix, Arizona along with three rescue pets - two dogs and one cat. In his spare time, Tim likes to hike and photograph the desert Southwest; enjoys eating Indian, Thai and Vietnamese cuisine; likes watching "Survivor" and any tattoo reality show; and follows the Pittsburgh Steelers, Pittsburgh Penguins and Arizona Coyotes.

You can learn more about Tim by visiting his personal website:
www.timcrum.com

To learn more about Tim's company, Animal Shelter Fundraising, visit:
www.animalshelterfundraising.com